Jeremy's Realization

Jeremy's Realization

When Jeremy's Truth Overtakes His Interruption

Jeremy Mutzabaugh

TREMENDOUS LEADERSHIP
Leadership with a kick!

JEREMY'S REALIZATION

When Jeremy's Truth Overtakes His Interruption

Published by:
Tremendous Leadership
PO Box 267
Boiling Springs, PA 17007

717-701-8159 800-233-2665

www.TremendousLeadership.com

ISBN: 978-1-949033-11-3

Printed in the United States of America.

DEDICATION

This book is dedicated to anyone (student or professional) who has ever wondered why things happen the way they do.

TABLE OF CONTENTS

INTRODUCTION

The first book I had published was titled *Jeremy, Interrupted*. In it, I talked about the challenges I had growing up as a learning-disabled student. Some of these challenges included things like: timed Math tests, getting static about my first prom date, and having a college roommate shoot off a gun in the middle of the night. I got through my rough times because I had a support system of wonderful parents, friends—and most importantly—a faith in God who I knew walked with me every step of the way.

"...I will never leave thee, nor forsake thee." (Hebrews 13:5)

What I wish to attempt in this second book is to describe a variety of events that I experienced after my schooling years had ended. These adventures, that I had the opportunity to go on, were full of sudden "interruptions" that happened along the way. How I handled these situations, and the realization I came to, is something I will share in the following pages of this book—*Jeremy's Realization.*

PREFACE

My hope with *Jeremy's Realization* is that my readers would know that our lives should not be centered on any one event. There are so many things that we experience in life—good and bad. Either way, it's important to know that everything has a purpose.

God's word promises that:

"...We know that all things work together for good to them that love God, to them who are the called according to his purpose." (Romans 8:28)

It's also important to note our attitude toward what happens to us in this life is essential:

> *"Let the peace of Christ rule in your hearts, since as members of one body you were called to peace. And be thankful."* (Colossians 3:15 NIV)
>
> and
>
> *"There is no fear in love; but perfect love casts out fear, because fear involves punishment, and the one who fears is not perfected in love."* (1 John 4:18 NASB)

For example, I know too many people who do not wish to retire from their jobs because they, "would have to pay an early retirement penalty," or they "would have nothing to do," if they retired. They have so much fear in their hearts of what *might* happen.

I know that there is more to life than my job. I could find a million other things to do with my "at home" time than to believe the lie that, "I would have nothing to do." My job cannot and will not ever buy me happiness.

The bible says:

Delight thyself also in the Lord: and he shall give thee the desires of thine heart. (Psalm 37:4)

Another example would be traveling. I believe it's important to get out and see the world around you. We are here for such a short time. God made so many beautiful places for us to see and allowed humankind to create so many interesting things. Yet, many are afraid to leave their own home, or don't even have the desire to do so. Take a chance, go on an adventure, (even if it's around the block) I can guarantee it will change your life for the better!

Thank you for this opportunity to share part of my life's story.

If you like what you read, let me know.

God bless,
Jeremy

Chapter One

CHICAGO

One of the pastimes I truly enjoy is venturing out to see new things. Sometimes I get ideas from books or movies on where to go. Other times, people have told me where they've gone and what they've seen, and then I'm inspired to go there too. In the summer of 2003, I decided to go to Chicago, Illinois for a few days. I took the Amtrak from Harrisburg, Pennsylvania and arrived just after 9:00 a.m. at Union Station in the heart of the city. It was a long trip and I was sitting a lot for most of the 15 hours. After getting my suitcase off the carousel, I knew I would enjoy the walk to my hotel. I made my way up the escalators to Canal Street where all the taxis and buses were lined up to pick up the deboarding passengers.

The first thing I noticed as I stepped outside Union Station was the air. The smell of exhaust from the vehicles, the south branch of the Chicago river—the aroma a bit like the ocean at low tide—along with a combination of food smells, came to my nose. I think each city has its own flavor of fragrances—in my opinion—and I liked Chicago's. The people bustled around me, each going to a different destination. I paused, taking in the city before me. Each building had its own character—looking like silent statues reaching up to the sky—the Sears, or Willis Tower as they now call it, rose above the rest. I was pretty sure that would be one of my destinations.

I made my way down the street to the next intersection where I pulled out a detailed street map of the area. I saw that I was only about 3 city blocks from the Holiday Inn, where I had my reservations. It was a perfect summer day—

the sky was a beautiful blue with white fluffy clouds, and the temperature temperate. True to her nickname "the windy city," a stiff breeze blew against my side off of Lake Michigan, while I walked. I packed light, only staying for two nights, so my suitcase didn't weigh much and was not cumbersome, which helped to make the walk more enjoyable.

The traffic whizzed by me. As I headed south, I looked to my left and caught glimpses of other majestic buildings. I had to focus on where I was walking—I was distracted because the skyline of the city was so beautiful and something I'd never seen before.

After registering at the hotel, I checked out my room and unpacked my bag. Still having energy to burn—and being early in the day—I decided to take a walk. I enjoy walking. I'm in good shape, so traversing several miles around a city is not a problem for me. I've always thought I could see so much more by walking, rather than flying by in a taxi cab. I still needed to make up my mind for sure as to what I wanted to see in the city. This was such fun. Between buildings, eateries, museums, and Lake Michigan—there was so much to see—I have to admit I was mesmerized. I stopped at a hotdog stand and ordered two of Chicago's famous hotdogs. Oh my, were they good! Maybe it was because I had worked up an appetite from all my walking, but they really were delicious. As I sat on a park bench and enjoyed my dogs, I decided I wanted to see the Field Museum, the Sears Tower for sure, and I also wanted to take a boat ride on Lake Michigan to see the city from the water.

The next morning, I woke up early and headed out to the Sears Tower. I wanted to be there early to avoid the massive amount of tourists that come to see the tower during the day. When I first arrived, I couldn't help but notice what a great job the caretakers did with the bushes and flowers at the entrance. Having majored in Ornamental Horticulture in college I saw their work and enjoyed the selection of plants and shrubs.

After I paid for my ticket to see the city from the Skydeck—along with several others—I enjoyed the informative videos while waiting for the elevator. The Skydeck is on the 103rd floor. The Sears Tower itself is 110 stories tall. The seven floors above the 103rd floor are for all the machinery it takes to keep the building running. I entered the elevator with a group of other tourists. As we began moving at about 18 miles an hour, I could feel my ears pop on the way up.

Once we arrived, everyone got in line to step onto one of the four glass ledges. They are 10 feet by 10 feet and protrude about four feet from the edge of the tower. The ledges are a box of glass that extends out from the building where people can see through the floor to the buildings below, and round about them. It's an awesome experience to stand on the clear floor and look all around you at the sky, the city, Lake Michigan, and the ant like vehicles below. I have to admit, my heart was beating faster than normal and my palms were a little sweaty, but it was a great experience!

*****

My next adventure was going to the Field Museum. This is one of many museums to see along Chicago's lakefront—the Planetarium and the Museum of Science and Industry are some of the others. I wish I would have had more time to see them all.

It was late in the afternoon by the time I got to the museum. Although I was tired from walking so far, I was excited to see the exhibits that I had read about. I was especially looking forward to seeing Sue. Sue is a Tyrannosaurus Rex—one of the largest meat-eating dinosaurs that ever lived. It was impressive to see her skeletal structure up close and, along with many others I took several pictures of her.

Next on my agenda, was the famous taxidermy that the museum is known for. I spent several hours fascinated by two floors of stuffed animals including birds, snakes, bear, moose, deer and so many more animals. I think taxidermy is such an art form—especially after seeing the beauty of these preserved creatures—some over one hundred years old!

While I was there, I also checked out the Egyptian and Peru sections of mummies. Here I learned about ancient life through the bodies preserved in death. It was so interesting to see the mummified bodies of ancient people.

The Field Museum was a fascinating building to me, offering so much to see. My favorite part was the taxidermy and the preserved animals that were so beautiful. I will never forget all that I saw. I highly recommend it to anyone who has the opportunity to visit this city.

*****

Early in the morning the next day, I headed to the lake front to catch a boat tour with Chicago's First Lady Cruises. This cruise showed you Chicago's architecture with style. It was a beautiful boat ride and the guide really knew the history of each building. I enjoyed hearing the stories. It was a 90-minute tour, that seemed to last only minutes because it was so interesting. The cruise was full of history and information about the origin of many of Chicago's magnificent buildings.

*****

After the boat tour, I headed back to my hotel to check out and head back to Union Station. My departure wasn't for several hours, but I always like to be early. I was in the Great Hall, reminiscing about all the things I had seen and experienced, when a man and woman walked up to me. The moment I saw them I felt uncomfortable. They introduced themselves as being with a certain religious group. They immediately started to ask me questions about my faith. I was cautious with my answers, not knowing who they were or why they wanted to know so much about me. This was a rude interruption that happened in the middle of thinking of what a great time I had in Chicago.

After a couple minutes the conversation ended and they walked away.

After they left, I immediately began to think what a horrible end to a wonderful time. But then the truth of God's word came to me.

> *"Peace I leave with you; my peace I give you. I do not give to you as the world gives. Do not let your hearts be troubled and do not be afraid."* (John 14:27 NIV)

So, in the end, as I boarded the train for home, God's truth, my truth, came to my heart and overtook a rude interruption that would have otherwise ruined a wonderful vacation.

Chapter Two

MASSACHUSETTS

Several years ago, in October, I took a bus trip to Salem, Massachusetts. This trip was just a weekend tour. I have to mention that my interest in taking this trip came from being raised as a child celebrating Halloween. Although, I know some people are not for it, I always looked forward with excitement to dressing up in costumes and getting as much candy as I could.

Every weekend in October, Salem closes a few blocks of their main streets to cars. This is so people—in all kinds of costumes—can walk through the streets celebrating

Halloween. Also, during this time, there are vendors that set up tables and sell crafts or other home-made items. The restaurants usually have a very good business at this time. There is supposed to be a woman that has a business as a licensed witch and can cast spells, but she was not there on the weekend that I visited.

*****

On my first morning, I went downstairs very early to get a good breakfast. The hotel offered a complimentary morning meal with your stay, so I took full advantage of it. While I was eating my eggs and pancakes, I saw a woman leave the hotel before dawn. It was cold enough outside that most people were wearing wind breaker jackets as they walked down the sidewalk. I choked on what I was eating because I had never seen anything like what was walking past me in all my life. A woman walked right by me, wearing nothing but a fishnet body suit with no under garments. People were watching her as she walked past, out the door, and jogged away down the sidewalk. I thought it was odd how she was brave enough to make a public display dressing like that, then jogging away through the city. Although, this was quite a sudden interruption to what I thought would be an uneventful time in Salem, it made me think of Jesus and the woman at the well. Here, he didn't judge her for all her sinfulness, but encouraged her. If I would have had time to talk to this woman, I would have done the same. The truth of God's word is so awesome when it becomes your truth. It gives you such peace and makes you want to share it with others.

*****

Before coming home on Sunday, the bus stopped in Fall River at the Borden House. In 1891 Lizzie Borden had been accused and arrested for axing her father and step mother to death. At her trial, she was acquitted. Now, the public can take a tour of the house. All the same furniture is still there. It is set up the very same way as it was when the crime happened. I still remember the odd feeling I had while I stood for several minutes inside the house. I thought of Auschwitz, and Hiroshima (although I've never been there)—and wondered—does the land ever forget the horror that happened to it? This was a question that crossed my mind. It was as if I could tell something bad had happened the moment I entered the room.

Chapter Three

ATLANTIC CITY

Another time I took a day trip to the Jersey shore. I went to Atlantic City, New Jersey. We arrived very early in the morning and were to be back on the bus and leaving by 1:00 a.m.

After walking the boardwalk, and going to several casinos, I ventured away from the ocean and the rows of shops and casinos. I wanted to see more of the city and what it offered. So, I walked past the hotels, and casinos that lined the boardwalk and went across the street behind them.

After I had crossed the street at a traffic light and intersection, I noticed a woman on the sidewalk across from me. She crossed the street coming towards me in the cross walk and started asking me questions as she approached. As we walked together to the other side, I quickly found out that she was a street walker. One of the clues, was her repeated question of, "would you like to get a room?" I was kind of scared, having never experienced a woman offering me sex for money before. We reached the other side of the street and I took a deep breath and I simply said "no, I better not." She said, "okay, but would you have a light?" I said, "Sorry, I don't smoke." She walked away down the sidewalk. I felt bad that she was doing that type of work, but was not sure what to say to her to entice her out of doing what she did for a living. This was also the last time I took a bus trip like that. The interaction with this woman was scary, and I felt ashamed too. But still, the truth of God's word prevailed in my heart over the situation:

"Let us draw near with a true heart in full assurance of faith, with our hearts sprinkled clean from an evil conscience and our bodies washed with pure water." (Hebrews 10:22 ESV)

Chapter Four

KENTUCKY

In the spring of 2018, I took a trip to Noah's Ark in Williamstown, Kentucky. This structure is made from all wood and uses the real-life measurements of the Ark mentioned in Genesis. On the first floor are wood boxes, and pens that the animals could have lived in. The top floor had rooms where the family could have slept. Also, there was a room that must have been a kitchen. There were rooms where people could have worked in—a blacksmith room for metal bending, and animal shoes was one that I enjoyed.

The tour that I took, also included a stop at the Creation Museum. This building is a self-guided tour. It allows you to venture through biblical history, stunning exhibits, botanical gardens, a planetarium, zoo, and also a zip line adventure course. It has paintings, bible verses, and life-like displays of people from the Bible. There is a display of Jesus' open tomb after he walked out of the grave. There is also a whole wing of the building designed like The Garden of Eden—there are also real trees and a real body of water. There are a couple of life like silicone displays of Adam and Eve, and these were the displays I liked the best. I really liked this museum and left the place with a feeling of happiness, knowing that just as death exists, so does life and creation.

Chapter Five

THE POLICE ACADEMY

In the spring of 2003, I took a Citizen's Police Academy course offered from a local township police department.

I had an interesting event happen several years before attending this Academy—this helped spike my interest in taking the course. What happened was a local girl had gone missing between her eleventh and twelfth grades of school. Someone saw her walking away from her car one evening and she was never seen again.

Several years after this happened, a farmer said they found some personal items of the girl in a stream on their property. A search team was organized, with our State Police leading the search. There was a large group of people gathered on that morning to search the side of a local mountain. I volunteered to be one of the searchers.

We walked and climbed the steep, hilly area. Climbing down ladders, we went into cement tombs in the ground from an old cemetery. The police had brought a couple of K9 dogs too, to smell for anything odd. It was interesting to see all that was involved in searching for a missing person.

We spent most of the morning searching for items that might have belonged to this girl, but nothing came about from the search. No one has seen her since the night she disappeared. I thought it was a good experience to help with this, but I still feel sad that this happened to her. There are still too many unanswered questions about it. I pray that someday the case gets solved and the girl gets found one way or another.

*****

The experience of being involved in the search for a missing person motivated me to attend the Citizen's Police Academy. For eight weeks, a small group of us would meet at a local police station and real officers would teach us. They showed us—by projectors, videos and notebooks—what an average day as a police officer would look like. A detective showed us how they questioned suspects.

We also had a tour of a county prison. When we were at the prison, we walked in the hallway right past the cells of the inmates. The policemen instructed us that we were to stay in a single file line and not look or talk to the prisoners. This was hard because as we walked by them, they called out to us and said things you would not want to repeat.

We also had a tour of the county's emergency management dispatch center where people called in and then help was sent to the caller's home. We also went to a magistrate's office and saw a "mock trial" of a suspect pleading a case against a police officer.

One session included a hands-on firearms class where we stood in front of a film screen and shot a real pistol filled with blank bullets at videos of people who were hurting other people. Then we went outside the building and saw a live hand grenade explode. The officer pulled the hook from the bomb, and tossed it away into an empty field. When it exploded, we could see red and then blue smoke filter up into the sky.

At the graduation from the academy I was presented with a top gun award for my good shooting skills. I was very proud to receive recognition for my skills at marksmanship and will never forget being honored in this way. All in all, I was glad I took the training because it broadened my knowledge of police work and

I would recommend it to anyone interested in learning more about the police men and woman who work hard to help, and protect us.

This Academy gave me a better knowledge of what officers do every day and made me realize that I am glad I shied away from that type of work! It does take a special type of person to be able to handle the dangers of this field.

Chapter Six

BE ENCOURAGED

On my trips and at the police academy, there were wonderfully memorable times—like when I received an award for my marksmanship, but there were also scary moments that were hard to understand. The bible gives me truth that helps me know that even when I don't understand something, my Savior is with me and encourages me to "just do it" and run my race. God's promises tell me that with Him nothing is impossible.

> *"With man this is impossible, but with God all things are possible."* (Matthew 19:26 NIV)

and

Wherefore seeing we also are compassed about with so great a cloud of witnesses, let us lay aside every weight, and the sin which doth so easily beset us, and let us run with patience the race that is set before us.... (Hebrews 12:1)

I know that the words I use and the attitude I have can direct the type of day I will have. If I think of getting sick all the time—I will probably be sick. If I think badly, I will probably have a bad a day. I need to speak and think good things over myself and others. Reading the Bible and the promises of God help with this, so you can experience peace and health in your life.

"Surely goodness and mercy shall follow me all the days of my life: and I will dwell in the house of the Lord for ever." (Psalm 23:6)

I need to be careful who I associate with because this too can lead me in to a dark place. If I deal too much with the wrong people, I can lose my sense of peace and happiness. The Bible says to not be misled:

> *"Bad company corrupts good character."* (1 Corinthians 15:33 NIV)

> *He that walketh with wise men shall be wise: but a companion of fools shall be destroyed.* (Proverbs 13:20)

I really think it is important to keep solid connections with your friendships. Life is short and fast and I think it would be sad to sever your friendships just because you graduate from school or retire from your career. Do your best to keep your friendships strong and if you have dropped contact with someone, try to reach out to them again.

*****

Over the years I've found some good ideas that have helped me—I hope they help you too.

1. People decide their habits, and their habits decide their future.

2. Sometimes we have to stay silent in an argument or walk away from people before we fall into a bad place.

3. Always look to strengthen your chain of friends and keep your current friendships and relationships strong.

4. Find ways to make new friends.

5. If you are not helping or serving other people then you are missing out on life.

6. What does not change your life for the better is not necessary in your life.

7. If you ever come to a crossroads in your life, pray about your issue and then take action, but most of all, always follow your heart.

Thank you, readers, for this opportunity to share with you. May God bless your dreams with peace.

*****

There are several bible verses that have helped me over the years to stay at peace. I know that even if I am going through a dark time. I can still keep faith and know that at some point I will come out of a bad situation. There is a nice sense of peace we can experience even as we go through our darkest days. There are times when we may get concerned about something, but we need to work through these issues so our concern does not lead us into depression.

> *Even though I walk through the valley of the shadow of death, I will fear no evil, you are with me.* (Psalm 23:4 NASB)

> *But I know that even now, God will give you whatever you ask.* (John 11:22 NIV)

Take delight in the LORD, and he will give you the desires of your heart. (Psalm 37:4 NIV)

And we know that God causes all things to work together for good to those who love God, to those who are called according to His purpose. (Romans 8:28 NASB)

Be very careful, then, how you live—not as unwise but as wise, making the most of every opportunity, because the days are evil. (Ephesians 5:15-16 NIV)

"I am coming soon. Hold on to what you have, so that no one will take your crown." (Revelations 3:11 NIV)

"Peace I leave with you, my peace I give unto you: not as the world giveth, give I unto you. Let not your heart be troubled, neither let it be afraid." (John 14:27 KJV)

Readers, we are victors because God has already defeated death; we too will defeat death. Satan has already lost and when the devil reminds you of your past, remind the devil of his future.

I hope you too let the truth of God's word overtake the sudden interruptions in your life. Once you realize this, I can guarantee from my own experiences, that you will have a much more peaceful and fulfilling life.

ABOUT THE AUTHOR

Jeremy Mutzabaugh is a native of Central Pennsylvania whose training is in Forestry, Conservation, and Ornamental Horticulture. He has also taken classes at the Citizen's Police Academy through a local police department. He likes promoting safety. Jeremy works doing manual labor and has a passion for serving and helping others. He enjoys the mountains, horses, traveling, learning new things and meeting new people. Jeremy is the author of another book: *Jeremy, Interrupted.*